STRETCH YOURSELF TO BETTER HEALTH

STRETCH

YOURSELF
TO BETTER
HEALTH

A Basic Stretching Guide to Help Relieve Headaches,
Sore Lower Arms And Lower Back Pain

NANCY HILKER

Illustrations by **Dallas Weimer**

Dedication

This book is dedicated to all my clients, who over the years have learned the value of stretching and now lead a better, less painful life. It is also dedicated to all my readers, who will now have the ability to live a more pain-free life with just a little stretching.

Contents

Stretching the most out of these pages

Please, treat this book like the tool it is meant to be.

Take this book with you to work and use it as a reference in the middle of a headache day.

Mark the stretches that work best for you.

Do whatever it takes for these stretches to become part of your life as you become more pain-free.

Introduction

Do you get **Headaches**?

Do you have **Sore Lower Arms**?

Do you suffer from **Lower Back Pain**?

This book is filled with stretches that will help these three problems!

At forty years old, I became a massage therapist and started my third health profession. At the time, I did not realize the impact I would have on my massage clients' lives. I also did not expect to practice massage for as long as I have. Most massage therapists practice an average of five years before injury forces a change in professions!

The stretches in this book are the ones I have been teaching my massage clients for the last twenty-four years, and I practice what I preach. I stretch after every massage I give and several other times in the day. Stretching has given me the longevity I needed to sustain a massage profession for more than two decades. Stretching your body's muscles is as important as strengthening those same muscles.

I have also discovered that we humans prefer quick fixes. This book is sort of a quick fix pill for three of our most common problems, Headaches, Sore Lower Arms, and Lower back Pain.

The story below, about lower back pain, is a perfect example of what stretching can do.

I have a massage client, Corey, who came to see me for a massage after his wife took him to the hospital with a "bad back".

He had tweaked his lower back and could not move. The doctor at the hospital said it was "just muscular" and gave him a prescription for muscle relaxants. Two hours later, he was on my massage table.

I worked on his lower back and needed his wife's help to get him up and off the table. He left that day using a walker to get to their vehicle. Two days later, I saw him again for a massage. He walked with a cane, and he had seen his chiropractor the previous day.

The massage went well, and he felt better at the end of it. At this appointment, I suggested a couple of stretches for him to try. The next day was a breakthrough day. As he stretched his lower back, it went click, click, click, click! He felt a huge relief from the pain.

The next day he arrived at his massage appointment, driving his own vehicle and walking fully upright—he had no pain. He felt his pain relief was due to the massage and the stretching. He continues to stretch often to keep his back pain free.

Now, one year later, Corey reports that in the morning before the start of his day, if he is stiff, stretching helps him get out of bed.

Corey also is an active snowmobiler and snowmobiling in the Rocky Mountains can be taxing on the body. So, before and after each time he goes out, he does several shoulder and back stretches, which keeps him on the snow, with his snowmobile, having fun.

The stretches in this book are just a few of the available options to try; many variations exist. At one time or another, I have practiced all of these stretches, and I've tried to make them easy to do.

Stretches are meant to be held for ten to twenty seconds. Muscles easily remember how short they can be but often forget how long they can be! Holding the stretch helps the muscle remember how long it can be.

If you were working out in the '80s, it was common to bounce while holding a stretch. Please do not do that; just hold the stretch steady. Our muscles have receptors that guard against overstretching. If you bounce during a stretch, these receptors say, "No, no, no, I don't want to get longer!"

Be gentle when stretching. Stretch until you feel the stretch, and then hold for ten to twenty seconds. As your muscles get used to being stretched, they will get longer, and you will find stretching easier or more comfortable. It will take a little time, but the investment in stretching your body will help you become healthier.

Disclaimer

The author, this book, and these stretches are not designed to replace medical advice! Before starting an exercise or stretching program, please check with your doctor to make sure it is the right program for you.

SECTION 1:
HEADACHES

If you experience headaches regularly, you will find the stretches in this section helpful.

Headaches can originate at the base of the skull, but the pain often radiates over the top of the head and sits at your forehead or eyes. Headaches can also start in tight and stiff neck or shoulder muscles.

Check the FIX IT GUIDE at the end of this section for the stretches that match your specific problem.

HEAD AND NECK STRETCHES

HEAD

You have muscles on your head, believe it or not! Stretching these muscles by massaging the head, especially the temples, is the easiest way to stretch these muscles. Give yourself a good scalp massage when you are washing your hair; this will help relieve tension in the muscles on your head.

NECK

The neck is another matter. Many neck muscles are designed for moving the head but also designed for holding the head up. If the pain from a headache is in the back of the neck, stretching the back of the neck is easy. If the pain from a headache is in the forehead and eyes, stretching the upper part of the shoulders will help.

All of these stretches are done either sitting in a kitchen-type chair or standing with your arms at your side.

NECK STRETCHES

STRETCH 1 – LOOKING DOWN

This stretches the back of your neck. If you have a stiff neck along your spine or a headache that starts at the back of the neck, this is a great stretch. You may find holding this stretch a little longer or repeating this stretch more often helps reduce the pain or burning in the neck or upper back.

- Look straight ahead
- Tuck your chin in
- Drop your head down by looking at your chest
- *Hold* for 10 seconds
- Bring your head up, look straight ahead
- *Repeat*

STEP 1

STEP 2

STRETCH 2 – LOOK AT YOUR ARMPIT

This is my favourite stretch, and it stretches the side of the neck and upper back. You may also feel the stretch down the side of your spine and shoulder blade. It is a great stretch to use if you have been sitting at a desk all day, gaming for hours, or looking at your phone.

- Look straight ahead, then look left
- Now look down at your left armpit
- *Hold* for 10 seconds
- **Repeat on the other side**
- Look straight ahead, then look right
- Now look down at your right armpit
- *Hold* for 10 seconds

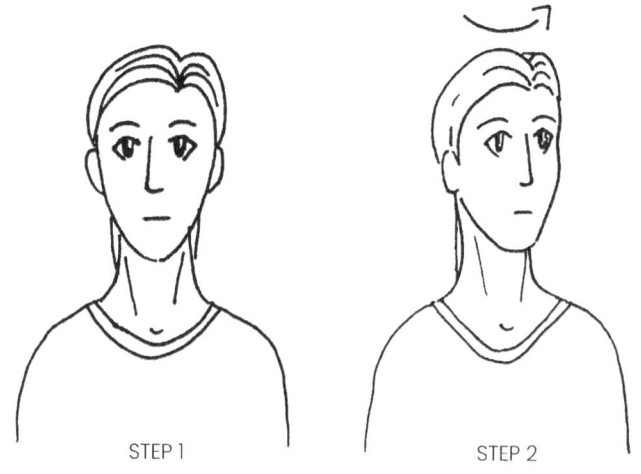

STEP 1   STEP 2

STEP 3

Looking down at the left armpit stretches the right side of the neck and upper back.

Now do the same thing looking at the right armpit.

STRETCH 3 – LOOK TO THE SIDE AND UP

You will feel this stretch on the front side of your neck.

- Look straight ahead
- Now look right and up
- *Hold* 10 seconds
- Repeat on the other side
- Look straight ahead
- Now look left and up
- *Hold* 10 seconds

STEP 1

STEP 2

STEP 3

STRETCH 4 – POUR WATER OUT OF YOUR EAR

This stretch is great for stretching the side of your neck and top of your shoulder. Be aware of your shoulders; keep them both down. Do not lift the shoulder being stretched up towards your ear!

- Look straight ahead
- Drop your ear towards your right shoulder as if your pouring water out of your ear
- *Hold* 10 seconds
- **Repeat on the other side**
- Look straight ahead
- Drop your ear towards your left shoulder as if pouring water out of your ear
- *Hold* 10 seconds

STEP 1   STEP 2

POUR WATER OUT OF YOUR EAR VARIATION:

Clasping your hands behind your back while doing this stretch helps keep your shoulders down and can promote a deeper stretch in the neck and shoulder area.

SHOULDER STRETCHES

Stretching and loosening the muscles around the shoulder helps relieve tension and tightness that cause headaches. This next stretch, which I call the door-frame-stretch, is one of my favourites. I do this stretch daily!

STRETCH 5 - DOOR-FRAME-STRETCH

Using a door frame as a tool allows you to stretch the front and back of the shoulder, chest, and front of the upper arm.

HINT: Start by standing in the hallway, then move to the inside of the room to stretch the other arm.

FRONT OF THE SHOULDER

You will feel this stretch from your chest, along the arm down to your wrist.

- Stand facing the door frame at arm's length
- Grab onto the door frame at shoulder height with your right hand, thumb up
- Turn the front of your body away from the wall
- *Hold* 10 seconds
- **Repeat with the other arm**
- Go to the other side of the door frame
- Stand facing the door frame at arm's length

- Grab onto the door frame at shoulder height with the left hand, thumb up
- Again, turn your body away from the wall
- *Hold* 10 seconds

As you hold onto the door frame, turn away from the frame to stretch the front of your chest and arm.

BACK OF THE SHOULDER

This stretch is designed to stretch down your shoulder blade and next to your spine

- Stand facing the door frame at arm's length
- Grab onto the door frame at shoulder height with your right hand, thumb up
- Relax your right shoulder
- Scoot your buttocks back like you are trying to sit in a chair

- *Hold* 10 seconds
- **Repeat with the other arm**
- Move to the other side of the door frame, inside the room
- Stand facing the door frame at arm's length
- Grab onto the door frame at shoulder height with your left hand, thumb up
- Relax your left shoulder
- Scoot your buttocks back like you are trying to sit in a chair
- *Hold* 10 seconds

DOOR FRAME VARIATION:

You can change the muscle being stretched at the back of the shoulder by moving the hand's height as it holds the door frame. If you move the hand up the door frame to above the shoulder, you will feel the stretch down low on the shoulder blade. Then move the hand holding the door frame down to below shoulder height, and you will feel the stretch higher up on the shoulder blade.

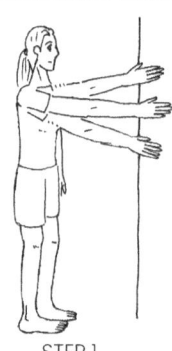

STEP 1

Select the height on the door frame, where your hand will be

STEP 2

Scoot your buttocks back like you are going to sit in a chair. Feel the stretch in the back along your shoulder blade.

STRETCH 6 – SHOULDER SHRUGS

These can be done sitting at a desk or kitchen-type chair or standing.

- Let your arms hang at your side
- Lift both your shoulders up to your ears
- Let your shoulders drop
- Do this 10 times

STRETCH 7 – BEAR HUGS

When you have pain and burning in your upper back, another stretch to relieve it, is a big bear hug. Do this stretch standing, sitting at your desk, or in a kitchen-type chair.

- Wrap your arms around your chest
- Touch your right hand to the left shoulder and left hand to the right shoulder
- *Hold* 10 seconds
- **Now switch which arm is on top**
- *Hold* another 10 seconds

BEAR HUG VARIATION:

While doing the big bear hug, look down and get a deeper stretch in the neck and upper back

STRETCH 8 – ANGEL ARMS

When I was a kid, in the winter we would make snow an-gels in the snow or sand angels in the sand in the summer. Moving your arms from your side to over your head mak-ing angel arms is the action of this stretch. This stretch re-laxes and activates the muscles of the upper back, giving relief from tight, sore, achy, or burning upper back muscles.

This stretch can be done standing or sitting in the kitch-en-type chair.

- Stand with your arms at your side, thumbs turned out
- Raise your arms above your head, slowly
- *Hold* at the top for a count of three
- Lower your arms, slowly
- *Repeat* 5 times

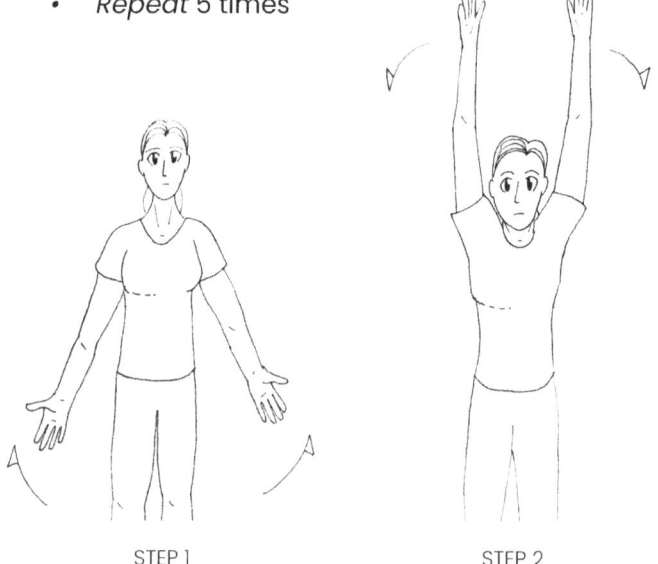

STEP 1   STEP 2

BACK OF UPPER ARMS

STRETCH 9 – ARM ACROSS THE CHEST

This stretch can be done sitting or standing and will stretch the back of the upper arm and the muscles around the shoulder blade.

- Bring your straight left arm up and across your chest
- Put your right hand on the left elbow
- Pull right hand towards the right shoulder
- *Hold* 10 seconds
- **Repeat with the other arm**
- Bring the straight right arm up and across your chest
- Put your left hand on the right elbow
- Pull the left hand towards the left shoulder
- *Hold* 10 seconds

SECTION 1 FIX IT GUIDE

STIFF NECK OR PAIN IN THE NECK

- Neck Stretch 1, 2, 3, 4

HEADACHES IN YOUR EYE

This headache can be caused by a tight upper trapezius (upper trap)—the muscle on

top of the shoulder. When the upper trap is tight, the referred pain comes from

the back of the skull over the top of the head to your forehead or eyes.

- Neck Stretch 4
- Back Stretch 5, 6, 8

HEADACHES AT THE BASE OF THE SKULL

The upper traps attach at the base of the skull. When you are stressed, and your shoulders

are up around your ears, the upper traps pull on the base of the skull.

- Neck Stretch 1
- Back Stretch 6

TIGHTNESS, PAIN, OR BURNING IN THE UPPER BACK

- Neck Stretch 1, 4
- Back Stretch 5, 6, 7, 8, 9

TIGHTNESS, PAIN OR BURNING ALONG THE SHOULDER BLADE

- Neck Stretch 2
- Back Stretch 5, 7, 8, 9

Section 1 Notes

SECTION 2:
SORE LOWER ARMS

Sore lower arms—from the elbow to the wrist—often result from the many things we do for work or recreation.

The carpal tunnel is at the heel of your hand, going toward the wrist. The nerves of the hand go through this tunnel from the forearm to the hand. When the muscles and tendons of the hand and wrist get tight or swollen, they put pressure on the carpal tunnel and may cause tingling or numbness in the hand.

Repetitive movements often cause carpal tunnel syndrome. This injury is often seen in office workers who type all day, in assembly-line workers putting the same part into the same hole hour after hour, in grocery store clerks pushing groceries across the scanner day after day, or in massage therapists massaging with the heel of the hand massage after massage. These are just a few examples of repetitive type jobs that can cause sore lower arms and hands.

Stretching the muscles in the lower arms, wrists, and hands can help keep pain and stiffness in the lower arms and carpal tunnel problems at bay.

I had the honour of teaching these next stretches to alarge group of office workers. Most of these women and men experienced stiffness or pain in their lower arms. Some had been diagnosed with the early stages of carpal tunnel syndrome.

I spent a couple of lunch hours going over how to do these stretches and teaching their value to the group. On a return visit, I learned that most of these women and men experienced less pain and stiffness in their lower arms and hands after doing these stretches regularly.

LOWER ARM STRETCHES

STRETCH 10 – BACKWARD HAND PULL

You will feel this stretch in your wrists and can be done either sitting or standing.

- Hold left arm straight out, palm up
- Take the right hand and gently pull the fingers on the left hand down toward the floor
- *Hold* 10 seconds
- **Repeat on the other arm**
- Hold right arm straight out, palm up
- Take the left hand and gently pull the fingers on the right hand down toward the floor
- *Hold* 10 seconds

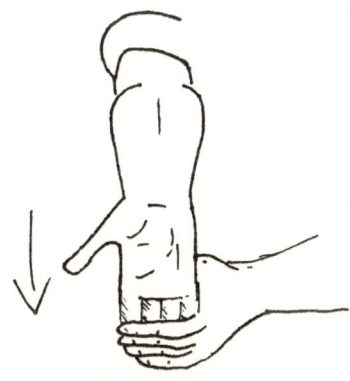

STRETCH 11 – BACKWARD HANDS ON THE TABLE

This stretch is also for the inside of the lower arm. I usually feel this stretch closer to the elbow. This stretch is done standing, both arms at the same time.

- Turn both palms up
- Stretch out all fingers
- Place fingers down onto the table, palm side down, fingers facing back toward you
- *Hold* 10 seconds

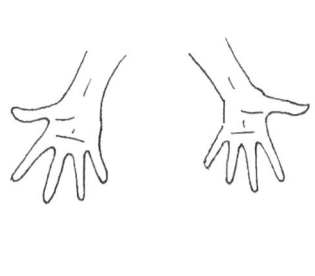

STEP 1

STEP 2
Try not to have your fingers hanging off the edge of the table

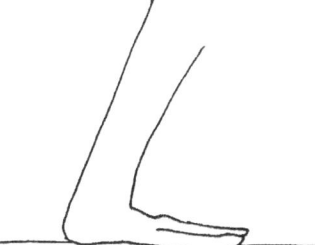

STEP 3
How close to the table your palms will be depends on how tight your hands and forearms are. This can be a deep stretch, so be careful!

STRETCH 12 – CROSS OVER HAND PULLS

This last stretch for the lower arm is one of my favourites and is designed for the outside of the lower arm. It is done standing. You will feel the stretch at the outside of the elbow of the lower hand.

I do this stretch often because my lower arms get very tight from massaging. I feel relief starting near the muscles at my elbow all the way down to my wrist.

- Arms straight out in front of you, thumbs turned down
- Cross right hand over the left hand, palms touching
- Clasp hands together by interlocking your fingers
- Left hand pulls the right hand until you feel a stretch in the muscles at the right elbow
- *Hold* 10 seconds
- **Change hands**
- Clasp hands together, left hand over the right hand, palms touching
- Right hand pulls the left hand until you feel a stretch in the muscles at the left elbow
- *Hold* 10 seconds

STEP 1

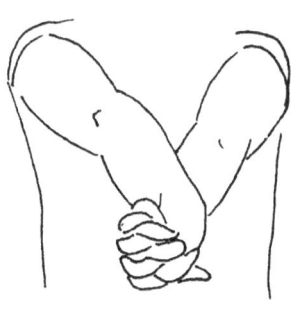

STEP 2

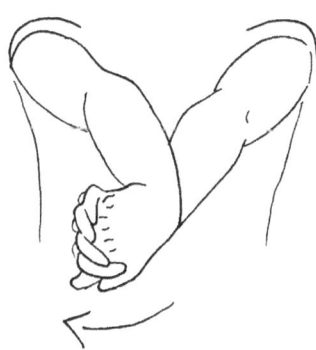

STEP 3

HANDS AND WRISTS

Your wrists have many tiny bones in them; by stretching your wrists and moving them around, your wrists become less jammed up and more flexible.

These next stretches can be done sitting or standing, both hands at the same time.

STRETCH 13 – WRIST ROTATIONS

Often when I do this stretch, I hear the sound of cracking in the wrists and feel a stretch in the elbows

- Arms stretched straight out in front of you
- Make fists with your thumbs tucked into the palm
- Rotate fists clockwise 10 times
- Then rotate fists counter-clockwise 10 times

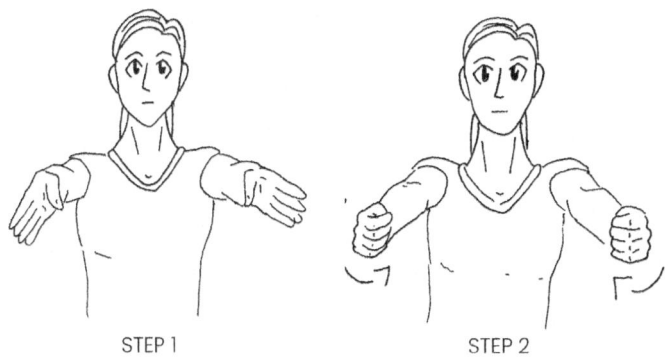

STEP 1   STEP 2

Rotate clockwise, then counter-clockwise

STRETCH 14 – HANDS UP, HANDS DOWN

- Arms stretched straight out in front of you
- Hands straight out with fingers and thumbs tight together
- Flex your fingers up then down 10 times

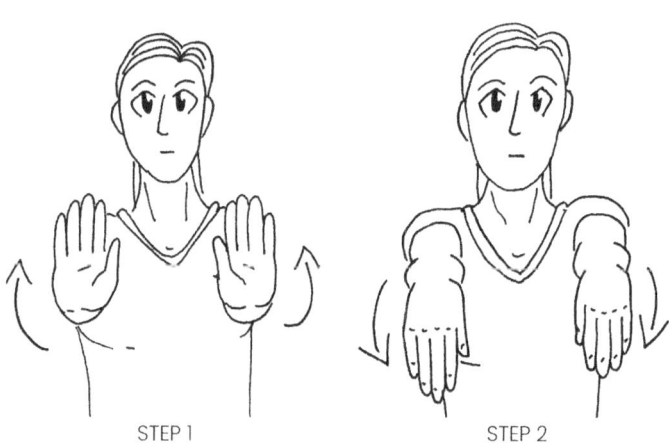

STEP 1   STEP 2

STRETCH 15 – HANDS SIDE TO SIDE

- Arms stretched straight out in front of you
- Hands straight out flat with fingers and thumbs tight together
- Move hands right then left 10 times

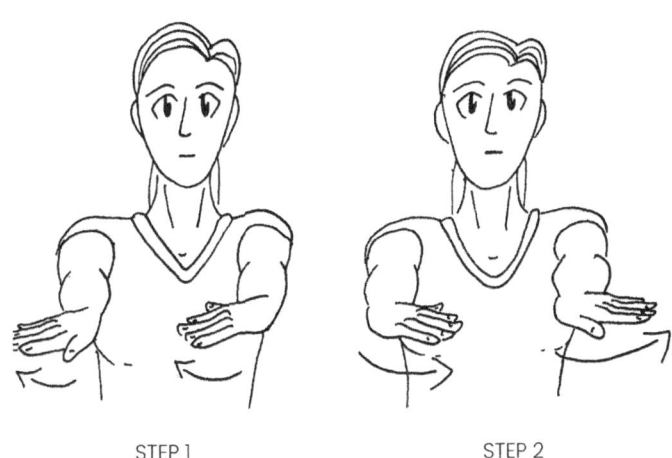

STEP 1   STEP 2

STRETCH 16 – MAKE A FIST

- Arms stretched straight out in front of you or to the sides
- Stretch fingers apart
- Make a fist
- Stretch fingers apart
- Repeat 10 times

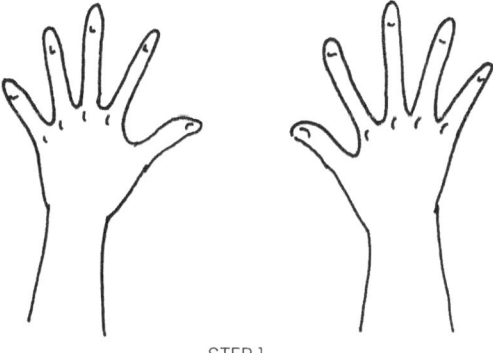

STEP 1

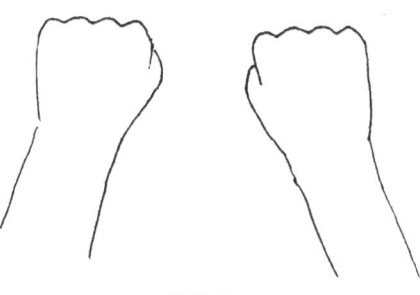

STEP 2

STRETCH 17 – SHAKE IT UP ARMS

- Arms above your head
- Shake your hands in all directions
- Shake for 10 seconds

This can be done sitting at a desk or standing. Do this when your hands, arms, or shoulders are tight and tired.

Many years ago, before I became a massage therapist, I worked as a receptionist at a dental office. I used to do this stretch a lot.

You may look crazy, but your hands, arms, and shoulders will feel awesome; so, close your office door and give your arms a good shake!

SECTION 2 FIX IT GUIDE

PAIN IN THE WRIST

- Wrist Stretch 10, 12, 13, 14, 15, 16
- Arm Stretch 10, 11, 12, 17

PAIN AT THE ELBOW

- Arm Stretch 11, 12, 17

PAIN IN THE LOWER ARM

- Arm Stretch 11, 12, 17

Section 2 Notes

SECTION 3:
LOWER BACK

Lower back tightness and pain often come from tight hamstrings—the muscles on the back of the upper leg—or tightness in the front of the hip. Both of these problems arise from sitting or standing for long periods.

My husband is a firm believer in these next stretches for the lower back. He injured his lower back early in his construction career, and he has been doing these stretches every day since. He likes to bend over and touch his toes in the shower and let the hot water pound on his lower back.

This stretch is easily done because it does not matter where your hands end up—thighs, knees, ankles, or toes. The key to this stretch is always drop your head down and look at your knees. This way, you will get a deeper stretch in the lower back and down the back of the upper legs.

BACK

STRETCH 18 – BEND AND STRETCH

- Stand up straight with your hands at your sides
- Bend over at the hips
- Reach toward your toes; go only as far as comfortable
- Remember to drop your head and try to look at your knees
- *Hold* 10 seconds
- Roll up *slowly* so that you do not get light-headed

Do not forget to drop your head and look at your knees

STRETCH 19 –COREY'S BACK STRETCH

This is the stretch my client, Corey, found so helpful when he tweaked his back and could not walk. While doing this stretch, Corey felt his spine go click, click, click, then the pain was practically gone!

You may feel this stretch along your spine from neck to lower back.

- Lay on your back
- Bring your knees up to your chest
- Place your hands behind your knees
- *Hold* for 10 seconds

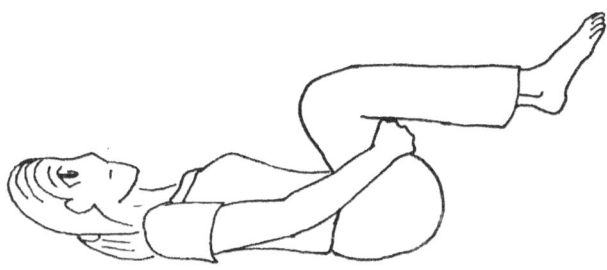

COREY'S BACK STRETCH VARIATION

For a deeper stretch, while laying on your back with your knees up and hands behind your knees, bring your head up.

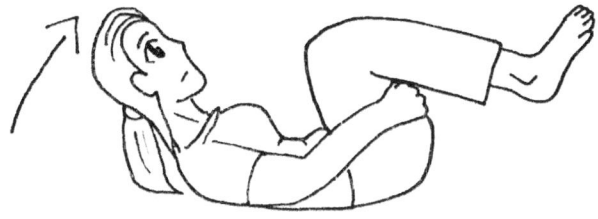

These next two stretches are for the front of the hip and work miracles for lower back pain, especially if you have been sitting for a long time. Deep in the belly, on the front and inside of the hip, is a muscle that runs from the pelvis through the body and attaches to the front side of the lower spine.

When you sit for an extended period, this muscle shortens and may rotate the pelvis forward. The problem is in the front of the body, but the pain shows up in the lower back region. That is why stretching the front of the hip is so important. Both, my husband, Greg and I love Stretch 20 – The Runner's Stretch.

STRETCH 20 – THE RUNNER'S STRETCH

- Get down onto the floor on your hands and knees
- Raise your upper body and hang onto a coffee table or the side of the bed
- Bring your left foot forward far enough to make a 90-degree angle at the knee
- Now sink your pelvis down toward the floor
- *Hold* 10 seconds
- **Repeat on the other side**
- Bring your left foot back so your kneeling
- Bring right foot forward, creating the 90-degree angle of the right knee
- Sink pelvis down toward the floor

This movement of shifting the pelvis is small but effective. You will feel the stretch in the front of the upper leg and possibly into the hip of the leg behind. Maintain the 90-degree angle of your bent knee so you do not put stress on that knee and ankle.

If you are doing this stretch on a hard floor, put a pillow under the knee to help protect it.

STRETCH 21 – STAIRS RUNNER'S STRETCH

For those who cannot get down on the floor, this is a variation of Stretch 20 – The Runner's Stretch and is done using stairs.

- Stand at the bottom of the stairs and hang onto the hand railing
- Bring left foot up onto the 2nd or 3rd step
- Keep your body upright
- Lean your pelvis into the stairs
- Again, keep the left knee at a 90-degree angle
- *Hold* 10 seconds
- **Repeat with the other foot**
- Bring right foot up onto the 2nd or 3rd step
- Keep your body upright
- Lean your pelvis into the stairs
- Keep the angle of your right knee at a 90-degree angle
- *Hold* 10 seconds

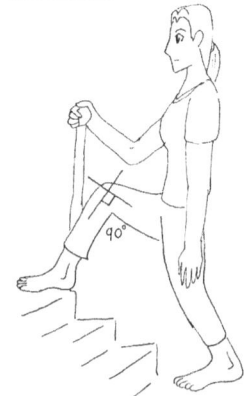

If you have long legs, you may have to use the 4th step up.

STRETCH 22 – HULA HOOP HIPS

I like to do this hula hoop movement when I have been standing for a long time, and my lower back feels tight. Think of yourself as a beginner hula dancer with a hula hoop around your hips.

- Stand with your legs hips distance apart
- Place your hands on your hips
- Move hips in a circular motion right, back, left, front
- Do five rotations clockwise, then five rotations counter-clockwise

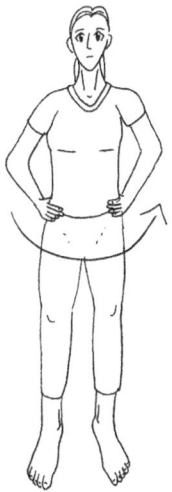

STRETCH 23 – CAT STRETCH

The Cat Stretch helps with lower back pain and stiffness from sitting or standing too long. This stretch is done on all fours on the floor. The movement can be small or large depending how flexible your lower back is. Breathing is very important in this stretch, so follow the breathing instructions carefully.

- Start by getting onto the floor on hands and knees
- Arms should be straight and under your shoulders
- Knees are at the 90degree angle
- Take a deep breath in and hunch your back, exhale
- Take a deep breath in and arch your back, exhale
- Repeat 5 times

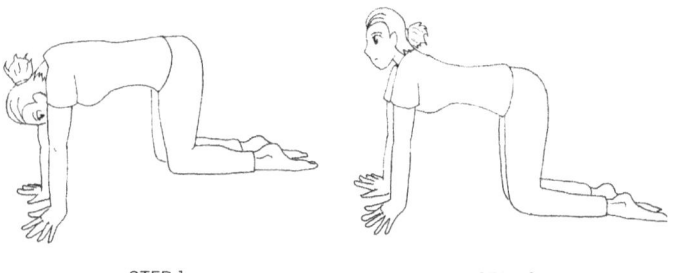

STEP 1   STEP 2

STRETCH 24 – SPINE TWISTS

Twisting the spine helps with lower and upper back pain. It also helps with spine flexibility.

- Sit in a kitchen-type chair
- Place your feet flat on the floor
- Your back is straight, arms hanging down
- Put your right hand on your left knee
- Look over your left shoulder, like you are shoulder checking when driving
- *Hold* 10 seconds, then as your back relaxes, rotate a bit more and look a little farther back
- *Hold* again for 10 seconds
- Return to face the front
- **Repeat on the other side**
- Put your left hand on your right knee
- Look over your right shoulder
- *Hold* 10 seconds, then as your back relaxes, rotate a bit more and look a little farther back
- *Hold* again for 10 seconds more

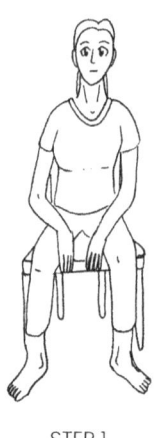

STEP 1

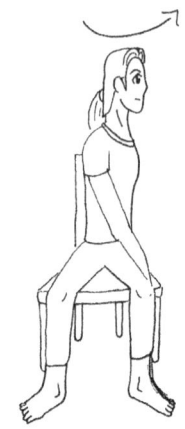

STEP 2
Look over your left shoulder

STEP 3
Look over your right shoulder

SPINE TWIST VARIATION

This spine twist can be done sitting cross-legged on the floor; it does not matter which leg is in front. Remember to hold each stretch for 10 seconds, then after your back relaxes, rotate a little further around and hold for another 10 seconds.

STEP 1   STEP 2

STEP 3

STRETCH 25 – SPINE STRETCH LAYING ON THE FLOOR

This spine stretch is a deeper stretch for the lower back and glutes.

HINT: This stretch can easily be done on the bed

- Lay on the floor on your back
- Arms straight out at shoulder height
- Left leg is straight, bend the right knee
- Bring the right knee over the left leg
- Look to the right
- *Hold* 10 seconds
- Bring your right leg back and straighten

- Right leg is straight, bend the left knee
- Bring left knee over the right leg
- Look to the left
- *Hold* 10 seconds
- Bring the left leg back and straighten
- Repeat three times on each side

GLUTES

Often stretching your glute muscles helps with lower back pain. The glute muscles are those in your butt. This stretch is done sitting in a kitchen-type chair or office chair, feet flat on the floor. This stretch may feel very awkward, but it is beneficial for stretching the outer hips and lower back. Stretch 23 – Ankle on the Knee Stretch is my favourite glute stretch.

STRETCH 26 – ANKLE ON THE KNEE STRETCH

- Place the left ankle onto the right knee
- With a very straight back hinge forward slightly at the hips
- Do not hunch your back when leaning forward—you get a better stretch in the lower back and glutes if you lean forward with a very straight back
- *Hold* 10 seconds
- **Repeat with the right foot**
- Place the right foot onto the left ankle
- Hinge forward slightly with a very straight back
- *Hold* 10 seconds

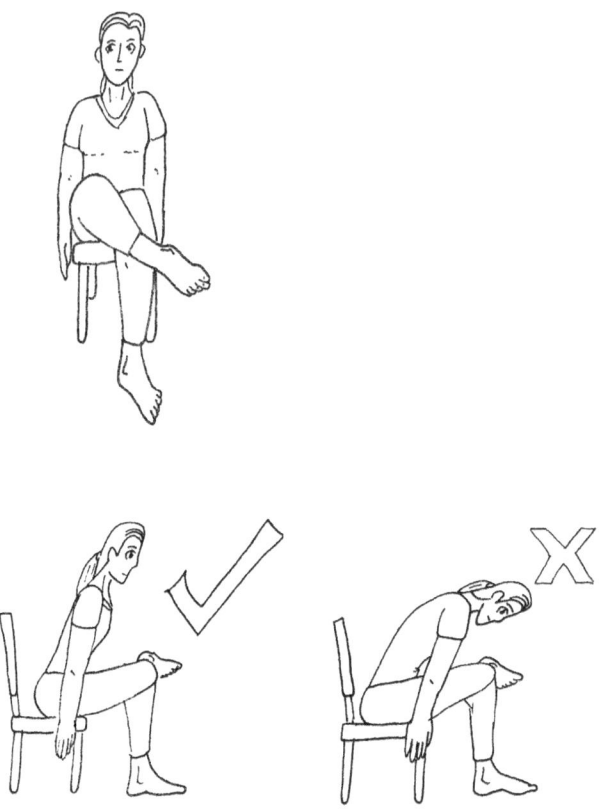

Keep your back *very* straight while you hinge at the hips; do not hunch.

ANKLE ON THE KNEE STRETCH VARIATION

If you cannot get your ankle on the opposite knee, try putting your ankle on the shin of the other leg. Be sure to straighten the leg you are placing the ankle on. Remember to keep your back very straight when you are hinging forward at the hips to get that great hip stretch.

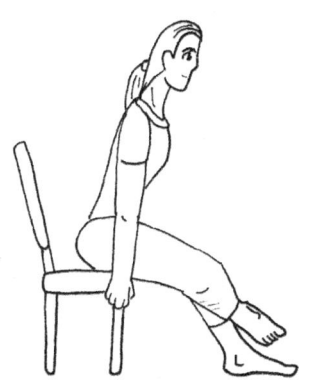

UPPER LEGS

FRONT OF THE UPPER LEG

The muscle group on the front of our upper leg is called the quadriceps or quads for short. The easiest way to stretch this muscle group is from a standing position. Stretching the quads is important if you have been sitting for a long time, as this muscle group can get very tight from sitting.

STRETCH 27 – QUAD STRETCH

If you need to, find a chair or wall to hold onto for balance.

- Stand on your left leg
- Lift right knee
- Grab your right ankle
- Pull right ankle back behind you and up toward your butt
- *Hold* 10 seconds
- **Repeat on the other side**
- Stand on your right leg
- Lift left knee
- Grab your left ankle
- Pull left ankle back behind you and up toward your butt

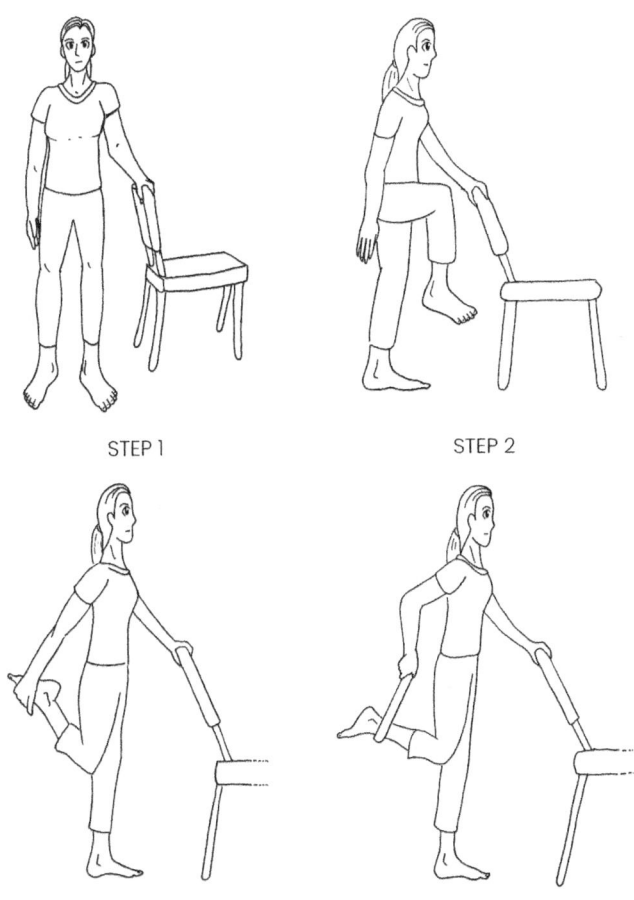

STEP 1

STEP 2

STEP 3
If you cannot grab your ankle with your hand, use a strap. Wrap the strap around the ankle and lift it toward your butt.

QUAD STRETCH VARIATION

For those of us, like me, with knee issues, this stretch option is a little easier on the knees because they do not get hyper-flexed.

- Sit on the floor with knees bent
- Lean back slightly, support yourself with your hands
- Flop your knees down to the floor to the left
- You will feel the stretch in the right quads
- *Hold* 10 seconds

- Bring your knees back up
- Flop your knees down to the floor on the right side
- Now you will be stretching the left quads
- *Hold* 10 seconds

STEP 1

STEP 2
Knees are open and stretching
the right quads

STEP 3
Stretching the left quads

BACK OF THE UPPER LEG

The muscle group in the back of the upper leg is called the hamstrings. They can get tight from sitting or standing for extended periods. This group of muscles can be stretched in many different ways. Here are three of the easiest.

STRETCH 28 – HAMSTRING STRETCH ON THE STAIRS

- Stand at the bottom of the stairs
- Hold onto the railing
- Put your left foot on the 3rd step up
- Keep your left leg straight
- Bend forward at the hips just until you feel a stretch at the back of the left leg
- *Hold* 10 seconds
- **Repeat on the other leg**
- Put your right foot on the 3rd step up
- Keep your right leg straight
- Bend forward at the hips just until you feel a stretch at the back of the right leg
- *Hold* 10 seconds

HAMSTRING STRETCH ON THE STAIRS VARIATION

If you have short legs or are not that flexible, use the 1st or 2nd step up.

STEP 1   STEP 2

STRETCH 29 – BEND AND STRETCH

This stretch stretches not only the back of the legs but also the back. This is the same stretch as Stretch 18 – Bend and Stretch

- Stand straight up, hands hanging at your side
- Bend over at the hips
- Try to touch your toes
- Remember to drop your head down and look at your knees
- *Hold* 10 seconds
- Slowly raise yourself so that you do not get light-headed
- You can touch your thighs, knees, ankles, or if you are very flexible, touch the floor. No matter how far you go, feel for the stretch down the back and in the hamstrings.

STRETCH 30 – SITTING TOE TOUCH

Settle your body back down on the floor

- Sit with your legs straight and feet shoulder-width apart
- Bend forward at the hips until you feel a slight stretch at the back of your legs
- You may also feel a stretch in your back
- *Hold* 10 seconds

SITTING TOE TOUCH VARIATION

For stability, place your hands on your thighs or on the floor outside of your knees as you bend forward.

If getting down on the floor is difficult, try doing this stretch sitting on your bed with your back against the headboard.

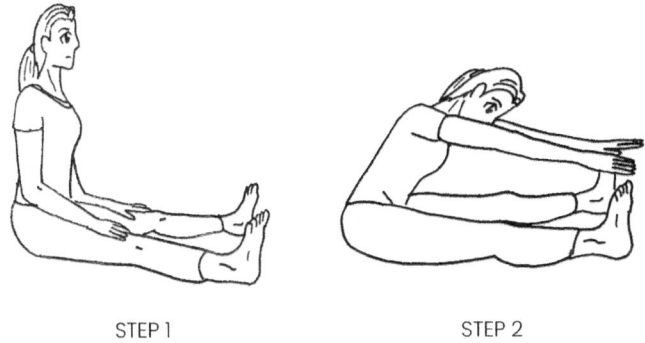

STEP 1   STEP 2

LOWER LEGS

The muscles in the front and back of the lower leg often get tight, tired, and sore from walking or changes in the heel-height of our shoes. Going from flat shoes to shoes with a heel, no matter how high, or from shoes to flip-flops or bare feet makes the muscles in the back of your lower and upper legs shorten. Consequently, this change is hard on the knee and hip joints and the muscles of the lower leg and lower back.

STRETCH 31 – WALL STRETCH

Stretching the back of the lower leg is best done facing the wall.

- Stand arm's length away from the wall with your hands on the wall
- Left foot in front, right foot behind, heels flat on the floor
- Bend left knee until you feel a stretch in the back of your right lower leg
- *Hold* 10 seconds
- **Repeat with the other leg forward**

HINT: If you do not feel a stretch in the back leg, move the back leg further back or away from the wall until you feel a stretch.

STEP 1   STEP 2

STRETCH 32 – TOP OF THE FOOT ON THE FLOOR

A muscle runs from the front of the knee down toward the foot then underneath the foot at the arch. This muscle is responsible for flexing the foot upwards during walking. So, with extra walking, this muscle can get very tight, sore, and even cause shin splints.

This stretch *must* be done without shoes on. It is awkward to do but well worth your while.

- Stand with your feet slightly apart while holding onto a table or counter
- Bend the right knee slightly
- Place the top of the left foot on the floor, slightly behind you
- Your toes will be pointed backward
- You will feel the stretch up the shin and front of the lower left leg
- *Hold* 10 seconds
- **Repeat with the right foot**
- Stand with your feet slightly apart
- Bend the left knee slightly
- Place the top of the right foot onto the floor, slightly behind you
- *Hold* 10 seconds

You will probably not get more than your toes onto the floor. That's okay if you're feeling the stretch up the shin. To get a deeper stretch up the shin, bend the supporting leg more.

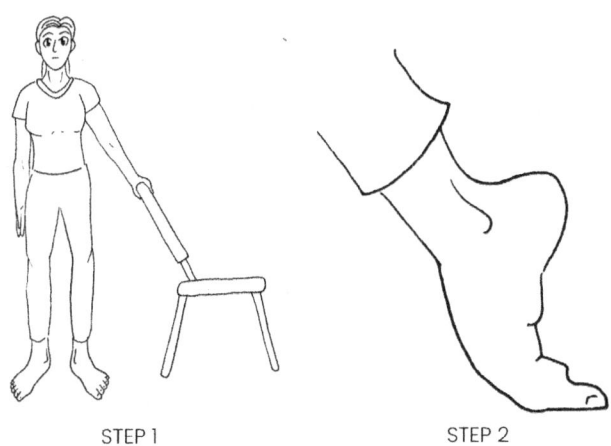

STEP 1   STEP 2

ANKLES

Ankle rotations help crackly ankles feel better. My right ankle cracks all the time due to a figure skating ankle injury. I find that ankle rotations somewhat help alleviate the crackliness. I tend to do ankle rotations unconsciously whenever and wherever, standing or sitting.

STRETCH 33 – ANKLE ROTATIONS

- Stand with your feet slightly apart
- Hold onto a table or counter
- Stand on your left foot
- Point the toes of your right foot down
- Touch the floor with your right foot toes
- Move your toes in a clockwise direction five times
- Change direction, *rotate* your toes in a counter-clockwise direction five times
- **Repeat on the left foot**
- Stand with your feet slightly apart
- Hold onto a table or counter
- Stand on your right foot
- Point the toes of your left foot down

Touch the floor with your left foot

Move your toes in a clockwise direction five times

Change direction, *rotate* your toes in a counter-clockwise direction five times

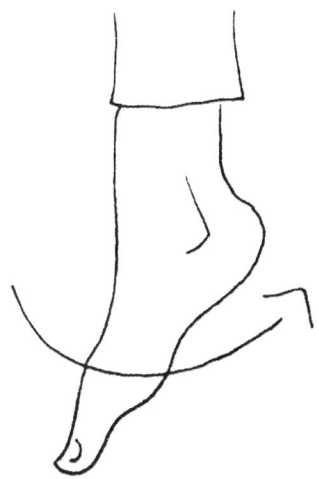

Rotate your toes in a clockwise then counter-clockwise direction

STRETCH 34 – POINT AND FLEX

- Stand on the left foot
- Raise your right foot slightly
- Point the toes of your right foot down
- Flex your toes up
- Point and flex 10 times
- **Repeat on the other foot**
- Stand on the right foot
- Raise your left foot slightly
- Point the toes of your left foot
- Flex your toes up
- Point and flex 10 times

HINT: This can easily be done sitting in a chair behind your desk or at the kitchen table.

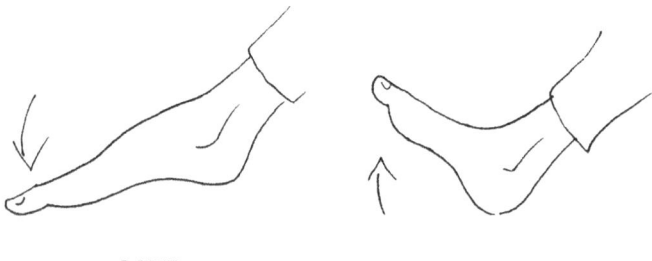

POINT   FLEX

SECTION 3 FIX IT GUIDE

PAIN IN THE LOWER BACK

If the pain is from sitting
- Back Stretch 19, 20, 21

If the pain is from standing
- Back Stretch 18, 19, 20, 21, 22
- Glute Stretch 24
- Leg Stretch 25

PAIN IN THE HIPS
- Back Stretch 22, 23, 24
- Glute Stretch 25, 26

PAIN IN THE UPPER LEGS
- Leg Stretch 26, 27, 28, 29, 30

PAIN IN THE LOWER LEGS
- Leg Stretch 29, 30, 31, 32

PAIN IN THE ANKLES
- Ankle Stretch 33, 34

Section 3 Notes

SUMMARY

Well, now you have stretched your body for your particular problem.

Your headaches are less severe. Working at the computer or playing your favourite video game is easier because your wrists and forearms do not hurt. Sitting, standing, or even exercising is not as painful because your lower back pain has lessened.

As you read through this book, if you did all of these stretches in order, it probably took you a while. Pick the ones that suit your needs best for the problem you have. Do not forget about the FIX IT GUIDE at the end of each section to determine the right stretches for you.

If you have a tight low back, you will not be able to touch your toes in one day. Do not push yourself too far. Your muscles have to adapt to what you're doing, adapt to the new you. Be patient and kind to your body.

Remember that muscles will remember how short they can be, not how long and stretched out they can be. Over time that muscle memory will change, and you will feel better. As a matter of fact, simple stretching may help you feel fantastic! Your body will love you for all the effort you have put into feeling better.

If you have questions about any of these stretches, please do not hesitate to contact me via email at **stretchyourselftobetterhealth@gmail.com.**

ACKNOWLEDGEMENTS

Greg Hilker: My husband of 32 years, Greg, has always been a huge supporter of everything I do. If I have a crazy idea, he always jumps in, headfirst with me. Thanks, honey!!!

Krysta Hilker: My daughter, Krysta, has a way of seeing things and putting everything into perspective. She gives honest feedback and lets me know if I am on the right track. Thank you for helping organize and produce all the social media. I could not have done that without your help.

Brett Hilker: You, my dear son, are the reason I am writing this book. You sparked the flame to write and have helped with the whole process. Thank you for all your help. I could not have done it without your encouragement.

Dallas Weimer: You have worked very hard at illustrating all the stretches in a way that makes sense. Thank you for all your help; I really appreciate it.

Corey Newman: I am very happy I was able to help you with your back problems. Thank you for allowing me to put your story into this book.

My Massage Clients: A special thank you to all my clients, who have listened, learned, and reaped the rewards of stretching.

Amy Colvin: Thank you Amy for making my words sound great and make sense. Your input, feedback and experience has made this book the version it is now.

Alejandro Martin: Thank you for all your hard work. Creating a great cover, then putting it all together to make an awesome book.

Self-Publishing School: The programs available through Self-Publishing School (SPS) allow someone like me, who has no writing experience, to write a book and get it published. With all the help available through SPS, it just takes an idea and the determination to get it done.

Made in the USA
Las Vegas, NV
07 March 2023